BOOK 2

Jazz Standards for Students

7 Graded Selections for Early Intermediate Pianists

Arranged by
Sharon Aaronson

Music in jazz styles ranges from original compositions to arrangements of well-loved "standards" from genres such as Broadway and movie music. These standards can be artfully transformed into jazz by adding syncopation, meter changes, heightened chord color, and improvisation. In this regard, jazz is often the end result rather than the beginning.

Jazz Standards for Students was written to introduce jazz styles to developing pianists at any age. Among the most popular styles represented in this series are blues, ragtime, swing, Latin, ballads, and the jazz waltz. The series includes jazz favorites that have become classics over the years such as "Satin Doll," "Blues in the Night," and "Duke's Place."

Jazz Standards for Students, Book 2, is arranged at the early-intermediate level with the pieces placed in approximate order of difficulty. Sixteenth notes and triplets are avoided; however, passages containing chromatic scales are explored. In addition to $\frac{4}{4}$ and $\frac{3}{4}$ time, $\frac{6}{8}$ meter is introduced. Key signatures contain no more than two sharps or one flat. The pieces in this collection are sure to bring out the jazz lover in any student!

Enjoy!

Sharon Aaronson

ALFRED

Produced by
Alfred Music Publishing Co., Inc.
P.O. Box 10003
Van Nuys, CA 91410-0003
alfred.com
Printed in USA.

ISBN-10: 0-7390-9046-1
ISBN-13: 978-0-7390-9046-6

BLUES IN THE NIGHT

Words by Johnny Mercer
Music by Harold Arlen
Arranged by Sharon Aaronson

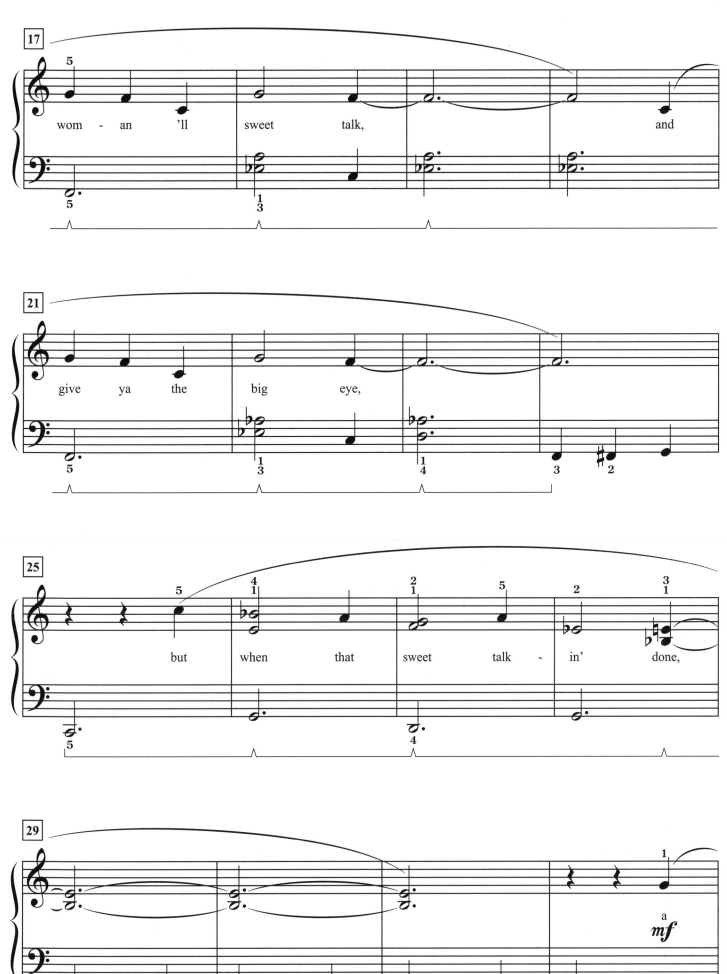

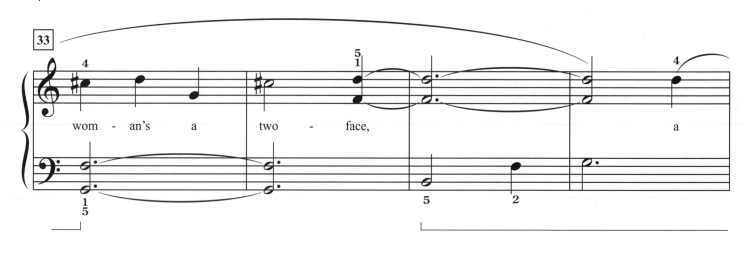

wom - an's a two - face, a

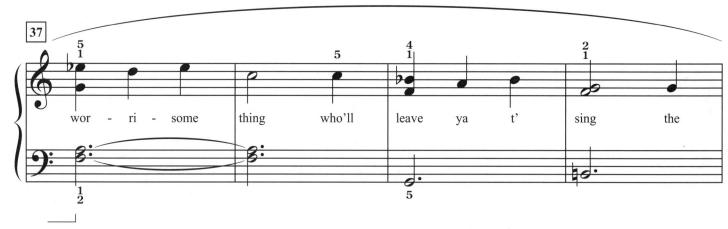

wor - ri - some thing who'll leave ya t' sing the

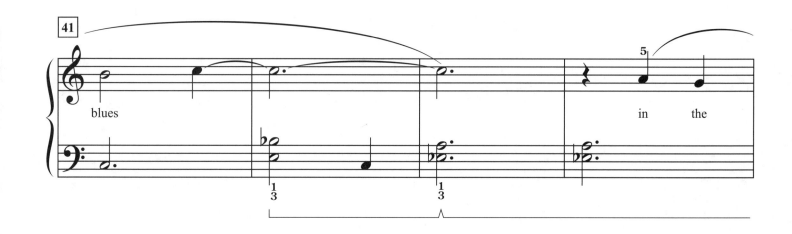

blues in the

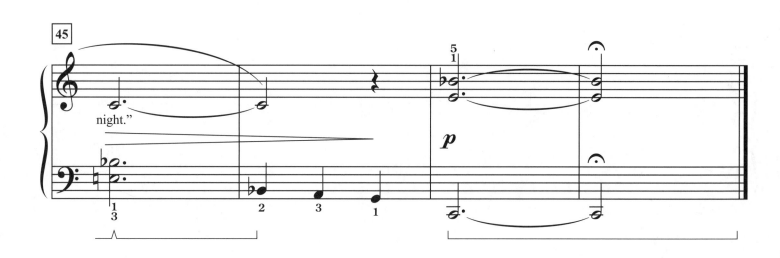

night."

SATIN DOLL

Words and Music by
Johnny Mercer, Duke Ellington and Billy Strayhorn
Arranged by Sharon Aaronson

speaks Lat - in, that sat - in doll.

She's no - bod - y's fool so I'm play - ing it cool as can

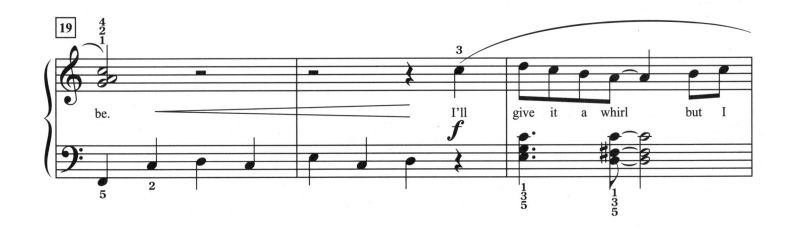

be. I'll give it a whirl but I

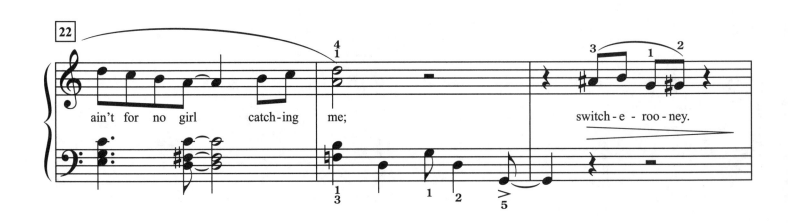

ain't for no girl catch-ing me; switch-e - roo-ney.

Tel - e - phone num-bers; well, you know, do - ing my rhum-bas

with u - no and that 'n', my sat - in doll.

And that 'n',

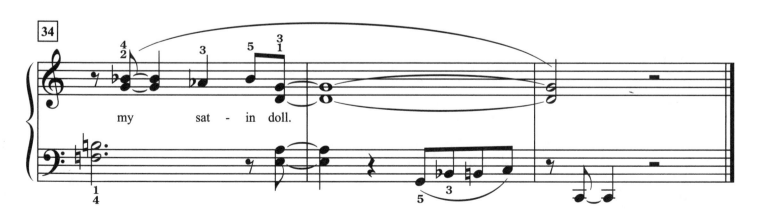

my sat - in doll.

DUKE'S PLACE

Music by Duke Ellington
Lyrics by Ruth Roberts, Bill Katz and Robert Thiele
Arranged by Sharon Aaronson

Fel-las swing their chicks at Duke's Place.

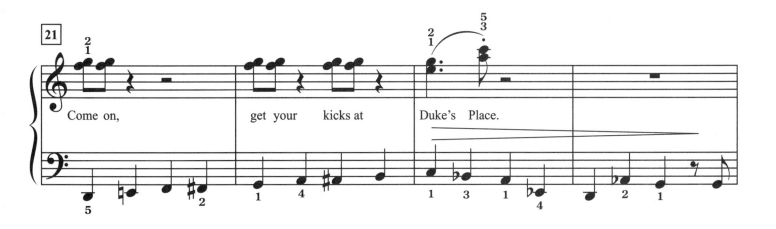

Come on, get your kicks at Duke's Place.

mp

dim. poco a poco

p

rit.

pp

FALLING IN LOVE WITH LOVE

Words by Lorenz Hart
Music by Richard Rodgers
Arranged by Sharon Aaronson

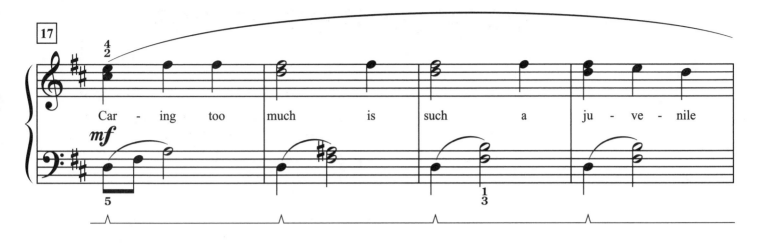

Car - ing too much is such a ju - ve - nile

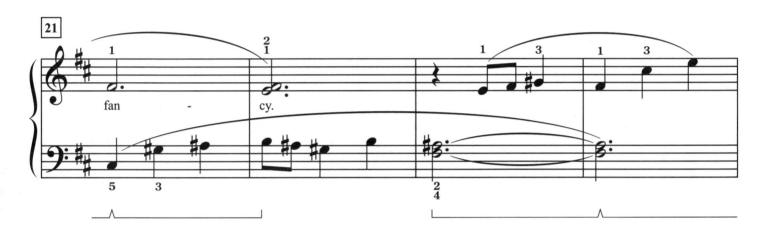

fan - cy.

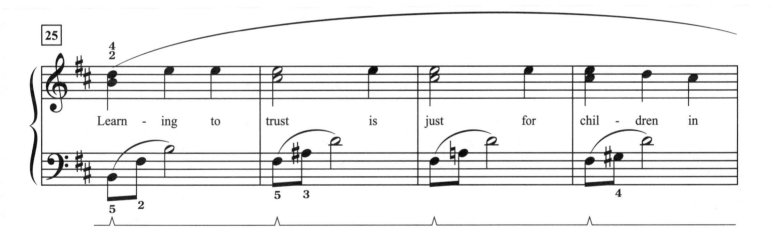

Learn - ing to trust is just for chil - dren in

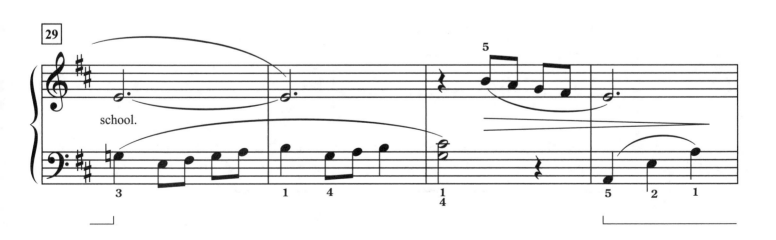

school.

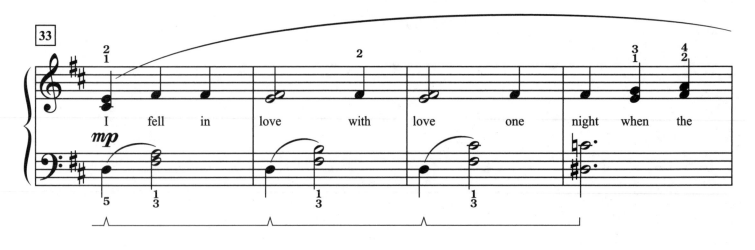

I fell in love with love one night when the

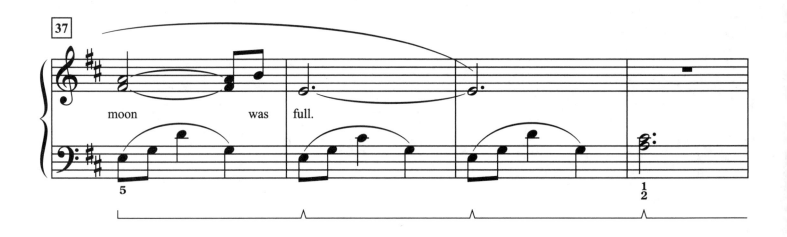

moon was full.

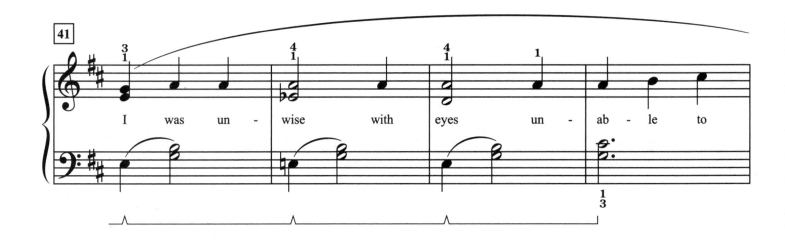

I was un - wise with eyes un - ab - le to

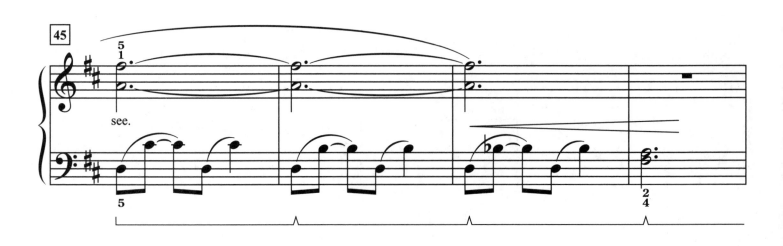

see.

CARAVAN

By Duke Ellington, Irving Mills and Juan Tizol
Arranged by Sharon Aaronson

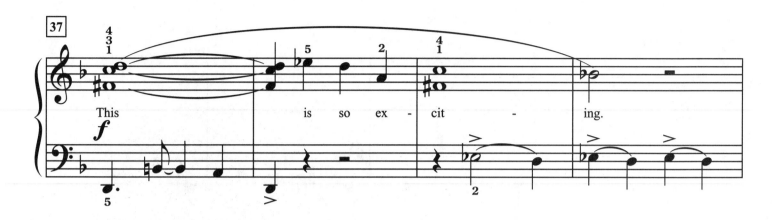

This is so ex - cit - ing.

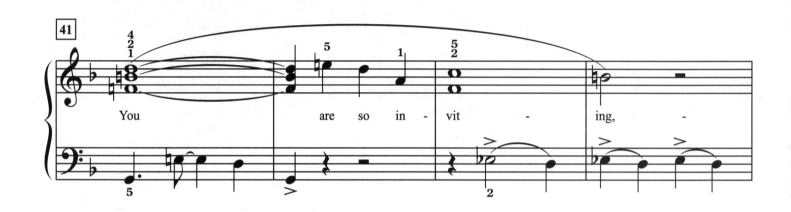

You are so in - vit - ing, -

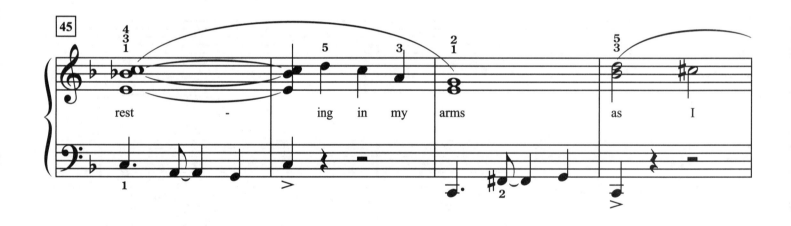

rest - ing in my arms as I

thrill to the mag - ic charms of

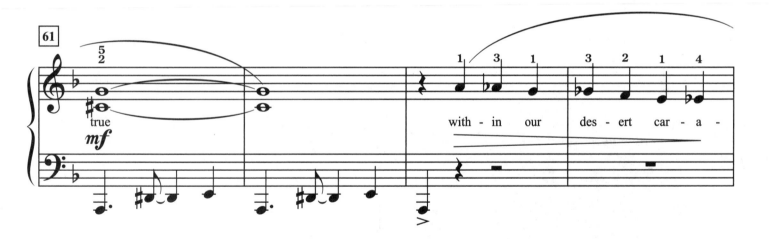

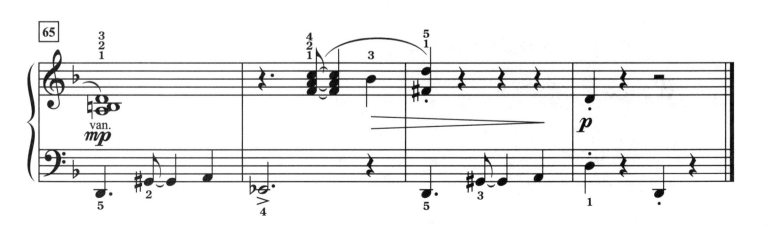

ST. LOUIS BLUES

Words and Music by W.C. Handy
Arranged by Sharon Aaronson

man   get   a   heart   lak   a   rock   cast   in   the   sea.

Or

else   he   wouldn't   have   gone   so   far   from   me.

Feel - in' to - morrow   lak   I   feel   to - day,

feel to - morrow   lak I feel to - day.

I'll pack my trunk,   make my get - a - way.

rit.

p

8va

A SUMMER BREEZE

(March and Two-Step)

By James Scott
Arranged by Sharon Aaronson

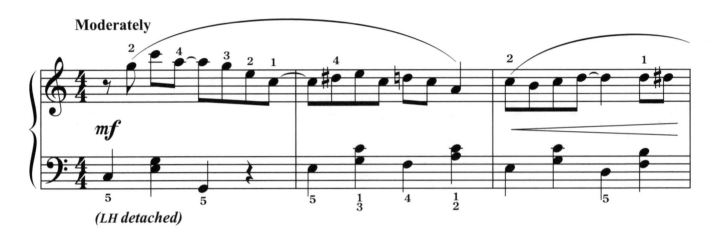

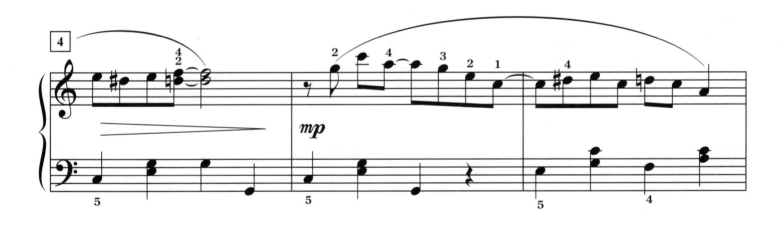

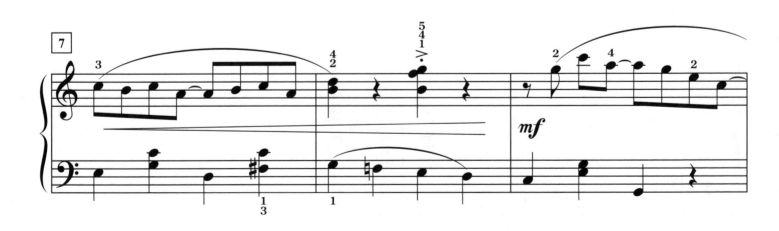

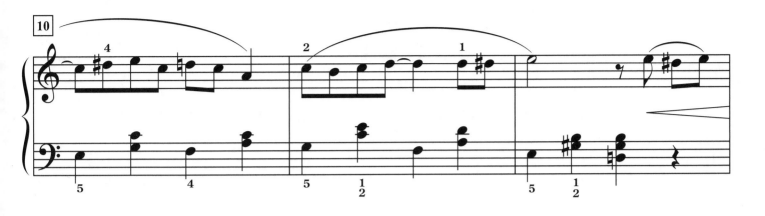

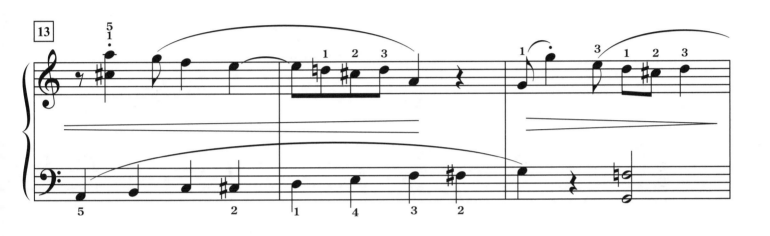

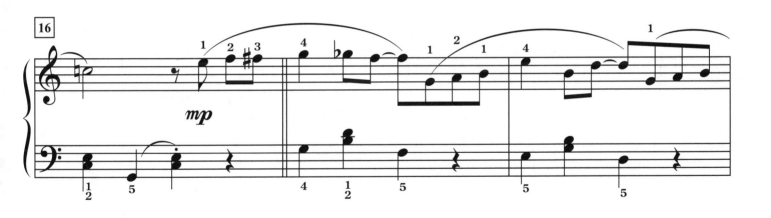

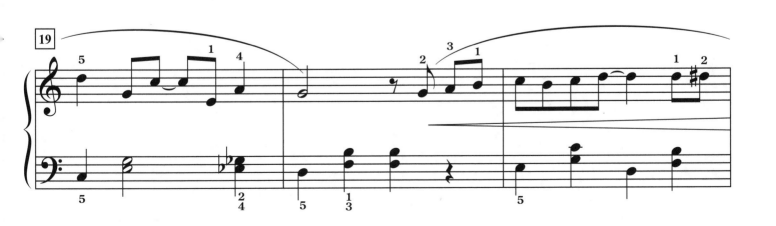